How to Build a 12 x 14
Hoop Greenhouse
with Electricity for $300

Jesse W. Love

Published by Kaleidoscope Productions
1257 Siskiyou Boulevard, Ste. 9; Ashland, OR 97520
www.kaleidoscope-publications.com

Cover design and book layout by 3 Wizardz
www.3wizardz.com

All Rights Reserved
Copyright © 2006 by Jesse W. Love

ISBN 978-1482035872

~Dedicated to~
My wife Sumara, my co-creator;
helping the garden of our lives together
to be abundant and fruitful.

OTHER BOOKS BY JESSE LOVE:

DEPRESSION FREE! HOLISTIC & MULTIMEDIA SELF-TREATMENT FOR OVERCOMING DEPRESSION WITHOUT DRUGS

HISTORY OF ST. AUGUSTINE
Whimsically Illustrated Account Of North America's Oldest City

HOT SPRINGS OF WESTERN WASHINGTON

11 SIMPLE CHOICES YOU CAN MAKE TO CHANGE THE WORLD

TABLE OF CONTENTS

Introduction..7
1. Frame and Rib Plan Overview..11
2. Materials and Tools Needed..13
3. Select a Site..15
4. Assemble the Foundation Boards...19
5. Place the Corner Posts..23
6. Assemble the End Frames..27
7. Assemble the End PVC Hoops..31
8. Assemble and Install Side PVC Hoops..37
9. Install the Plastic End Walls..43
10. Build the Door..45
11. Install the GFI Outlet, EMT Conduit and Wiring..................................49
12. Install the Roll-up Plastic Over the Hoops..53
13. Attach the Grommets and Place the Straw Bales..................................55
14. Operating Your Greenhouse..59

INTRODUCTION

Following is the step-by-step procedure to build a 12x14 foot greenhouse (168 square feet), with electricity for lights, fans and heat that can be built in one day, by one person, using common tools you probably already have in your tool box, along with some simple things like screws and door hinges from your local hardware store.

This is a variation with some important modifications, from a design I believe came originally from North Carolina State University. I built the modified version by myself in 10 hours, including laying the underground conduit for the electricity which had to have a 4-inch deep trench dug and run 60 feet from the house to the greenhouse.

This unit would be considered a small greenhouse compared to commercial greenhouses, but it is actually larger than most greenhouses available at stores for the home gardener. It's really quite spacious. I enjoy relaxing out in mine in a lounge chair reading a book amidst all my flowering plants on cold winter days when it's below freezing outside, but bright and sunny and a toasty 80 degrees in the greenhouse. Many bedrooms are about this size. Measure your bedroom and it will give you an idea of the greenhouse size in comparison.

Your greenhouse can be used for a lot of different purposes. In the late winter/early spring you can use it to germinate and start bedding plants and vegetables 30-45 days earlier than would be possible in open exposure without a greenhouse. In the summer it can be used with or without misting or self-timed irrigation to grow a variety of plants that like heat. The roll-up front feature assures it never

How to Build a 12 x 14 Hoop Greenhouse

gets too hot inside. In the fall you can use it to start winter vegetables and during the winter you can use it to protect hardy potted vegetables, flowers and patio plants from the sting of the cold nights.

The basic design is the same as the Rib & Frame Overview below with the addition of a 16-foot 2x2 that holds the plastic on one side of the greenhouse. The single sheet of 4 or 6 mil clear plastic that covers the greenhouse ribs is attached to the 2x2. As the greenhouse is 14-foot long, the 16-foot 2x2 will stick out 1 foot beyond the plastic on each end. This becomes the handles for roll-up front which will be detailed later. During the summer, the south wall of the greenhouse is designed to roll up on hot days, providing cooler air, more ventilation and stronger, less diffused sunshine, which is important in the cloudy Northwestern US where I built mine.

The second major modification is simply berming the perimeter base of the finished greenhouse on all sides with at least one layer of straw bales and piling them up 2 to 3 bales high on the north side of the greenhouse that never receives any sun anyway. Straw bales are inexpensive, super insulators, and this in effect makes a partially underground greenhouse, especially if you build up 2 to 3 layers on the north side. This is very effective at helping to maintain the warmth in the greenhouse during the colder days of winter. Place the bales narrow side up so rain drains through them if you want them to keep their shape, or wide side down if you want the rain to soak them so they will decompose in place.

The third modification is a recommendation to use Grip Rite Grip-Caps to fasten the plastic to the wooden frame rather than wide-head roofing nails or staples.

This is a strong structure and has no problem with the frequent 20-40 mph winds and even stronger gusts we often experience in the winter in Sequim, Washington, or the occasional snowfall. It gives me beautiful flowers year-round and delicious tomatoes and big, crunchy cucumbers from March 1st – November 1st. It has been a great investment and saved a lot on our grocery bills. It's amazing the quantity of vegetables you can grow in a 12x14 foot space. I love my greenhouse and I'm sure you'll love yours too!

To save time watering each day, I installed a small, automatic irrigation system for about $50.00 including the automatic timer and all the necessary tubing. This

Introduction

type of drip irrigation system is available at any hardware/garden store.

FRAME AND RIB PLAN

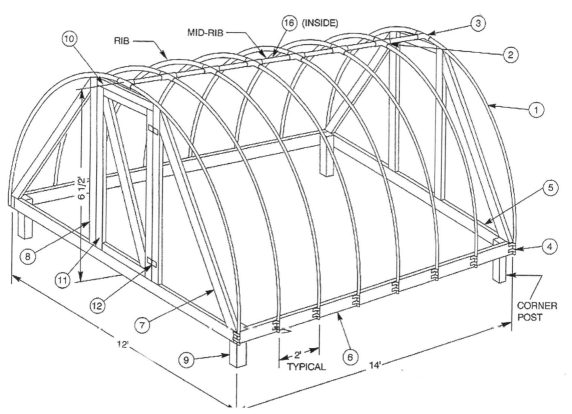

Figure 1 *Construction Details*

1. ¾" PVC Pipe

How to Build a 12 x 14 Hoop Greenhouse

2. ¾" PVC Crosses
3. ¾" PVC T's
4. ¾" EMT Straps
5. 2"x6"x14' Boards
6. 2"x6"x12' Boards
7. 2"x4"x86" Boards
8. 2"x4"x77" Boards
9. 4"x4"x15" Boards
10. 2"x4"x3' Boards
11. 2"x4"x70¾" Boards
12. 1 set of Door Hinges
13. Sheet of 24'x20' Plastic
14. omitted
15. omitted
16. ½"x10' EMT Tubing

MATERIALS AND TOOLS NEEDED

Quantity & Description

- Sixteen ¾" PVC Pipe, schedule 80, 10 feet long
- Six ¾" PVC crosses, schedule 80
- Two ¾" PVC tees, schedule 80
- Two 2"x6"x14' treated no. 2 pine or hemlock boards
- Two 2"x6"x12' treated no. 2 pine or hemlock boards
- Four 2"x4"x7' treated no. 2 pine or hemlock boards
- Four 2"x6"x6' treated no. 2 pine or hemlock boards
- Four 4"x4"x2' treated no. 2 pine or hemlock boards
- Two 2"x4"x3' treated no. 2 pine or hemlock boards
- Two 1"x4"x12' treated boards (to be cut up for door parts)
- One 16' 2x2 pine or hemlock
- One ½"x10' galvanized electrical metallic tubing (EMT) (ridgepole)
- ½"x however long you need, galvanized (EMT) tubing (wiring)
- One Circular or Hand Cross-cut saw
- One Electric or Hand-held Phillips Screw Driver
- One Carpenter's Square
- One Carpenter's Triangle

How to Build a 12 x 14 Hoop Greenhouse

- One 1' to 3' Level
- One 6' A-frame Step Ladder
- One Grommet Tool
- One Shovel
- Thirty-two ¾" galvanized electrical metallic tubing (EMT) straps
- One set of door hinges
- One box 1" Phil Mod Truss Lath Screws
- One box 7/16 Self-drilling Screws
- One box 6x3.5 Coarse Deck Screws
- One box 6x2 Coarse Deck Screws
- One box Grip-tite Grip Caps
- One roll Duct Tape
- Insulated 3 wire electrical cord to reach to GFI outlet from house
- Thirteen Straw Bales or more if insulating north face
- One Sheet of plastic, 24'x20', 4 mil (6 mil better)
- One Can of PVC Cleaner
- One Can of PVC cement

Note on angles: The cuts needed for the various pieces of lumber have the angles indicated. Most are 90 degrees with a few that are 45 degrees. A carpenter's square and a carpenter's triangle are very helpful tools to quickly insure your 90 and 45 degree angle cuts.

SELECT A SITE

Start by selecting a fairly level site, with good drainage and sufficient space to place the 12'x14' greenhouse plus a minimum of 5' of walk space on all sides as you will (optionally) be berming the outside base with straw bales. Try to choose a place where the soil is not too difficult to dig in as you will be digging holes for the four corner posts.

If you are going to use it to start seedlings or transplants in the spring or grow vegetable and flowers through the summer, you'll probably want to orient the 14' side facing south for the maximum sun exposure. In the Northwest, I need all the sun I can get so I also placed mine 60' from my house so there would be no shadows from the house falling on the greenhouse in the morning or late afternoon.

If you live in an area that has more than enough sun you may want to place your greenhouse where it can be partially shaded to help it from overheating in the summer and/or orient it with the smaller 12' side facing south. Overheating is less of a problem with this design than similar greenhouses, because you are able to roll the entire front half of the greenhouse plastic up to the roof ridge or less high as needed to keep the temperature just right. If you are growing plants that like heat but prefer shade, you can also put up a shade cloth to limit the amount of sun falling on the plants inside the greenhouse.

Finally, don't forget to place your greenhouse a practical distance from a source for water and electricity.

How to Build a 12 x 14 Hoop Greenhouse

Figure 3a

Figure 3b

Select a Site

Figure 3a & 3b show the level spot in a cut and dried hay field, about 60 feet behind my house (out of picture to the right). I temporarily placed the two 14' base pieces and one of the 12' base pieces in position to get an idea how the greenhouse will sit on the ground which is not perfectly level, full of rocks, and very hard to dig in. The far 14' piece is the south facing edge. My placement sloped downhill a bit to the east. This is easily compensated for with the corner legs which shall be described later.

Figure 3c shows another perspective of the site for my greenhouse in a hay field behind my house. The plastic wall (top left) is a wind shield for my existing garden.

This picture also shows all of the pieces of lumber, metal and PVC tubing that

Figure 3c

How to Build a 12 x 14 Hoop Greenhouse

will be used to construct the greenhouse, (except for the 2"x2"x16') laid out on a large sheet of weed blocking mat. All my plants will be in pots sitting on top of the weed mat rather than planted in the ground, as the ground is just too hard and rocky.

To make a greenhouse that will last for 8-12 seasons, (except for the plastic covering), you should only use lumber that has been treated with an environmentally safe preservative like CCA. For your own health and safety don't use lumber preserved with toxic chemicals like pentachlorophenol or creosote. Lumber that has been treated for ground contact will have a higher concentration of preservative than regular lumber. Technically that means it should last longer, but I preferred to go with regular treated lumber. It was cheaper, and I was happy to have fewer chemicals around the food I was going to be eating.

ASSEMBLE FOUNDATION BOARDS

Figure 4a

Weed matting laid over the ground where you will build your greenhouse is an optional step. Even though weeds will still poke through it over time I still recommend it as a non-toxic way to keep them at bay.

1. You can buy black weed matting in various widths from 3 feet to 10 feet. From whichever width you choose, cut sufficient pieces to make a piece 16x18, which

How to Build a 12 x 14 Hoop Greenhouse

Figure 4b

Figure 4c

Assemble Foundation Boards

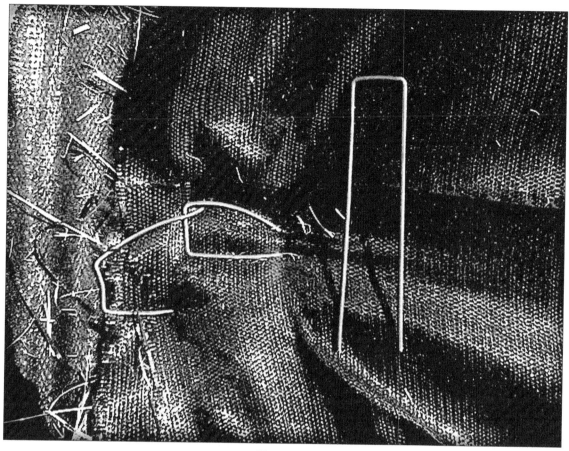

Figure 4d

will allow it to extend 2 feet beyond the perimeter of the 12'x14' greenhouse.

2. Affix the corners and outside edges of the weed matting to the ground with sturdy tent stakes as shown in *Figures 4b & 4c*. These come in various forms from thin metal ones to the thick yellow plastic ones. You can buy them at outdoor storcs.

3. Affix the inside edges of any strips of weed matting with the horseshoe shaped weed matting stakes as shown in *Figure 4d*, which you can buy at the same store you purchased the weed matting.

4. From your 4x4, cut four 15" pieces to use as the four corner posts.

5. Attach the posts to the two 14' foundation boards and the two 12' foundation

boards, with two 3" coarse drywall screws on each board corner, as shown in *Figure 4a & 4e*. All angles are 90 degrees.

Figure 4e

PLACE THE CORNER POSTS

Figure 5a

1. With the foundation assembled and placed in the position you want the finished greenhouse, pull the weed matting aside as shown in *Figure 5a* and raise up one

How to Build a 12 x 14 Hoop Greenhouse

corner sufficiently high to enable you to dig a hole directly beneath the corner post as shown in *Figure 5b*. You can use scrap lumber pieces to prop up the corner. Go at least 6" deep on every corner.

2. Next, using a 2' or longer level placed on top of the foundation boards as shown in *Figure 5a*, dig each corner hole deeper as needed to enable the foundation boards to all set level. Use the 2' or longer level to insure levelness along the foundation boards in both directions from the post. On my greenhouse, to compensate for the slight incline of the ground, my SE corner ended up being just 6" deep while my SW corner was 15" deep. The end result was perfectly level foundation boards.

If you happen to be building your greenhouse on a steeper slope, you can still maintain the overall level of your greenhouse by simply using longer corner legs on the downhill side and insulating the gaping space with additional hay bales.

Important: Make sure you use a carpenter's level on all 4 sides.

3. Once all four sides are level, dig each corner hole as deep as possible while

Figure 5b

Place the Corner Posts

maintaining level on all sides. The deeper the posts are the better the green house is anchored from high winds.

If you know your greenhouse is going to be a permanent fixture in this location you can even mix a little cement and pour it into the holes around the legs. Not only will this more firmly anchor your greenhouse from buffeting winds, it will also better protect the underground legs from moisture and rot.

4. The weed matting that had been pulled back away from the corner post must now be pulled back into position. As it will be extending beyond the corner post you will need to use some scissors to cut at a 45 degree angle from the corner of the matting, 28" in, so you can pull the matting around the post and anchor it with tent stakes to the ground, as shown in *Figure 5c*.

Figure 5c

ASSEMBLE THE END PVC HOOPS

Figure 6a

Some might wonder why the end hoops would be set up before the end framing. Admittedly this is an optional arrangement. If you prefer you could switch this step with the next and set the framing up first. However, after

How to Build a 12 x 14 Hoop Greenhouse

speaking with several people that have purchased this book in the past and built greenhouses, I discovered that though the measurements for every component are clearly spelled out, everyone was not as adept at making accurate cuts on their lumber. By putting the end hoops in first it gives some leeway if you do not make perfect cuts on your end framing pieces. With the end hoop as a guide you can, *if necessary* adjust the lengths of the lumber and cut to fit. I do not recommend this and would prefer you to cut to the length I have prescribed. But you do have some wiggle room if you don't, as long as your end hoop is in place.

It is fairly important that the size of all the hoops are uniform otherwise the plastic covering will not make a tight fit and the greenhouse will be more affected by wind and snow. It is for this reason that if necessary, it is better to adjust the height of the end frames to fit the hoop, than to have the hoops on the ends possibly be different heights than the hoops in the middle. Experience has also shown that it is easy to install the base of the pvc hoops by making them flush with the bottom of the foundation boards. But if you try to even out your hoops by placing the ends of the pvc pipe in varying heights along the foundation boards, it becomes an impossible puzzle to get it right. So once again, *if necessary*, it is better to adjust the heights of the end framing to insure hoop size uniformity.

Now some building professionals will be terribly upset with me giving you this option. However, though I believe it is entirely within everyone's capabilities to make all the lumber cuts in these directions as shown, reality has proven that is not always the case. I would rather you have a beautiful, functioning greenhouse that you built, even if all the cuts didn't end up being perfect, than to please the perfectionists that will be upset with me for giving you a way out in case you are not perfect. That said, let's get on to business.

1. Cut at 90 degrees and join two 122" PVC, schedule 80 pipes together with a PVC **T** joint. Use a fine-toothed hand saw or hack saw to cut the pipes and liberally apply PVC Cement (with ambient temperature above 50 degrees F) on the inside of the joint. (See ***Figure 6b***)

Note: The pipe seen coming in perpendicular in the ***Figure 6b*** picture is the ridge pipe attached later.

Assemble the End Pvc Hoops

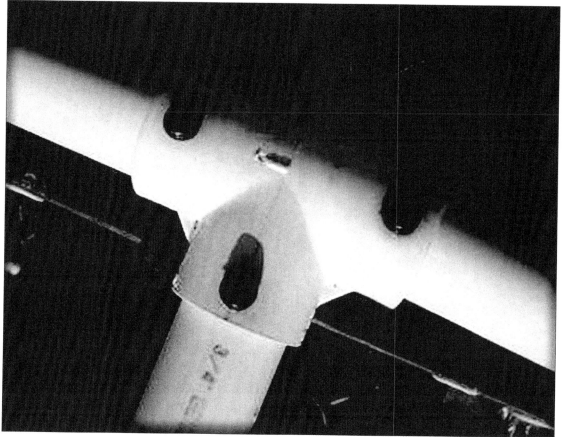

Figure 6b

2. Use 7x7/16 self-drilling screws to drill through T-Connector and into PVC pipe for a tight joint connection. You may want to use two screws, one on the top and one on the bottom side of the T-connector for each joint.

3. Loosely attach two EMT straps with 1" Phil Mod Truss Lath Screws to the end of the 14' and 12' foundation boards. (*See Figure 6c*).

4. Insert one end of End Hoop pipe into the EMT straps as shown in Figure 6c on one side of the greenhouse. Once in proper position, tighten EMT straps by tightly screwing in Lath Screws.

5. Repeat the procedure on the other side of the greenhouse, bending the pipe into an arch as you insert it into the EMT straps on the opposite side of the greenhouse.

How to Build a 12 x 14 Hoop Greenhouse

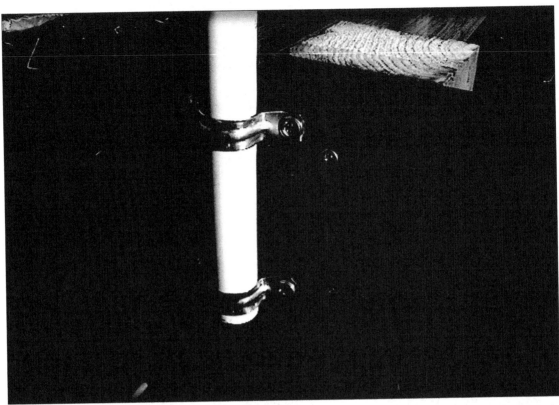

Figure 6c

6. Using the same steps outlined above, assemble the second End Hoop at the other end of the greenhouse.

ASSEMBLE THE END FRAMES

Figure 7a

How to Build a 12 x 14 Hoop Greenhouse

This is one of the trickiest parts of the entire greenhouse assemble especially if you are working alone, but it is still pretty easy if you support your framing as you put it up with temporary boards nailed to the frame. My instructions are based upon assembly by a single person. With a second person to hold and support pieces being assembled some steps could probably be eliminated. Please refer to **Figures 7a and 7b** for this step. The directions that follow are for one end frame. Simply repeat for the end frame at the opposite end. You may choose to have a door or not on the opposite end frame. Regardless, the framing itself is the same.

1. Cut and put in place the two vertical supports. The finished size for these will be 71", but at first cut them 77" so you can extend them along the 12' foundation boards and temporally tack them to the foundation boards with 2 sheetrock screws

Figure 7b

Assemble the End Frames

each. (*See Figure 7a*) *If you are working by yourself, it is helpful to temporarily block underneath the vertical framing with scrap lumber for support.*

Important: Use a carpenters square to insure your verticals are square at 90 degrees with the foundation board.

2. Trim the corners off the top of both vertical supports at an angle of 35 degrees.

3. Cut to a length of 86" and install the two diagonal supports using lath screws. The angle cuts are 45 degrees.

4. Cut the top horizontal support to a length of 36" with 90 degree cuts and install with sheetrock screws through the angle cut of the vertical supports.

Do not put screws on the inside of the verticals as they will interfere with the door opening.

Figure 7c

5. Liberally use your level and carpenters square to insure all pieces are properly positioned at exact angles. Otherwise you will have trouble installing your door.

6. Cut off the bottoms of the vertical supports at 90 degrees, so they rest on the top edge of the foundation board. Once done, firmly attach them to the foundation board with lath screws angled in from the outside. Do not angle in screws from the inside unless they are inset completely into the wood so they do not interfere with the door opening.

7. Cut two 2"x4"x3' pieces with 90 degree cuts, and using sheetrock screws attach them into the inside side of the vertical door frames with the base of each 3' piece firmly placed upon the ground. This will add additional strength on windy days.

8. From scrap 2x4's, measure two 3 1/2" lengths and cut two identical pieces with

Figure 7d

Assemble the End Frames

a 45 degree cut. Affix these as shown in **Figure 7c** to the top of the corner post and connecting to the bottom side of the diagonal end framing. This will give necessary support to the end frame.

9. Cut two pieces of 2x4 with 90 degree cuts to the length needed to place beneath the 12' foundation board and parallel with the 2'x4'x3' support as shown in **Figure 7d**. The length will depend upon how far your particular greenhouse is from the ground based upon the slope of your ground. Attach this piece with sheetrock screws to both the foundation board and the 3' support. This will give additional support to the 12' foundation board as people have a tendency to step on it as they come and go in the greenhouse.

ASSEMBLE AND INSTALL SIDE PVC HOOPS

1. Assemble the ridge pole by cutting 7 sections of PVC pipe with 90 degree cuts, each 22.5" long.

2. Clean all PVC cross joints and both ends of the just cut sections with PVC cleaner.

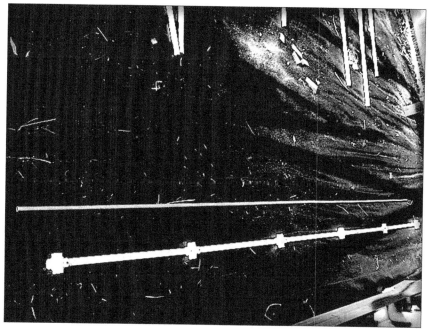

Figure 8a

How to Build a 12 x 14 Hoop Greenhouse

Figure 8b

Figure 8c

Assemble and Install Side Pvc Hoops

Figure 8d

3. Using the PVC cement, join 7 ridge pipe sections to 6 PVC 4-way cross joints as shown in *Figure 8a*, which is still missing the 2 pipe sections that join to the end PVC T joints.

4. Insert the 10' piece of EMT tubing into an open end of the ridge assembly. (See *Figure 8b*).

5. Using PVC cement and self-taping screws, attach the glued and screw fastened ridge pole to the ends of the T connectors on each end hoop as shown in *Figure 8c*.

6. Use two 7/16th self-drilling screws at each pipe end and joint connect to further anchor the joints as shown in *Figure 8d*.

7. Loosely install remaining 24 EMT straps along 14' foundation boards on each side of the greenhouse. Each end of a hoop needs 2 straps to secure it. Space the straps for each hoop about 4" apart and about an inch away from the top and bottom edge of the foundation board respectively. Each pair of straps should be centered 23.75" from the adjacent pairs. (14' foundation board divided into

How to Build a 12 x 14 Hoop Greenhouse

Figure 8e

7 sections less 2" taken away by straps on End Frame, 1" from each frame). (*See Figure 8e*).

8. Install 10' PVC pipe section of each hoop by threading one end through a loose pair of EMT straps then bending into the appropriate cross connector as shown in Figure 8f. Make sure both the inside of the connector and the outside of the pipe have been cleaned and liberally applied with PVC Cement. A second person is helpful for this step to prevent stressing the cemented joints.

9. Immediately after you have placed the end of the 10' PVC pipe section into a cross connector, firmly secure it with 2 self-tapping screws, one on top, and on one bottom.

Figure 8f

Assemble and Install Side Pvc Hoops

Completed Hoop Assembly

Fogure 8g

Notice on **Figure 8g** how short the uphill legs to the right are compared to the downhill legs to the left. The legs are actually all 15" but the uphill legs are buried further in the ground to compensate for the hill slope and create perfectly level foundation boards.

INSTALL THE PLASTIC END WALLS
(Please refer to Figure 9 below)

How to Build a 12 x 14 Hoop Greenhouse

1. You can use 4 mil or 6 mil plastic and also have a choice of clear, milky or white. Clear is best if you live in a cool, not very sunny area like the USA NW. Opaque or milky is a better choice in areas that have more sun as they reflect some sunlight and help keep the greenhouse cooler. If the greenhouse is going to be used exclusively for propagating or over wintering plants this color film is also a good choice as it limits the fluctuation of heat and light keeping conditions more constant. Any type of plastic deteriorates under the UV rays of the sun. After a couple of summers it will just become frail and brittle. However, 6 mil can last 2 seasons in areas with lower UV and is stronger in all areas.

2. You can choose to make the plastic on the End Frames single or double sheet. Double sheet is recommended, especially if you are using clear plastic. The extra layer doesn't appreciably decrease the sunlight entering the greenhouse and forms an air barrier between the sheets that adds insulating value in the later fall and early spring.

3. To make double sheet just cut a piece of plastic large enough to wrap around each triangle section and each end upper hoop section of the End Frames. Liberally use **Grip Tite Grip Caps** to fasten the plastic by hammering into the wood of the End Frames. Grip Caps are a far superior way to fasten the plastic than nails or staples as the plastic will not rip out during high winds or the weight of snow on the roof.

4. Make the plastic tight by hammering in a Grip Cap most of the way in, then grabbing the plastic behind the cap and pulling it tight while you hit the Grip Cap a few more times to push it down securely.

5. Cut the plastic large enough that it can extend onto the ground and out at least 2 feet on the outer side. The straw bales will sit on this extra flap, keeping them off the ground and helping to seal the base of the greenhouse tightly.

6. Using scissors, trim the inside plastic overlap after all your Grip Tites are in place on both sides.

Note: *Whenever possible do not attach the plastic in the same orientation plane it will be when it is installed, as even with Grip-tites it can still rip out. Always try to bring the plastic around at least one 90 degree turn on the lumber before attaching. Two 90 degree turns such as around the edge of a 2x4 support is even better.*

BUILD THE DOOR

Figure 10a

The door does not have to be anything fancy. Simple 2x2's and some scrap 2x4 end pieces for corner supports will be all that you need except two brass hinges, a little nylon rope to use for door handles on both the inside

How to Build a 12 x 14 Hoop Greenhouse

Figure 10b

and the outside and something to use for a latch. I used an old can opener. It is important to pick the straightest possible 2x2's when you are at the lumber store.

Remember the door has to be slightly smaller than the frame to account for any swelling, or if you are a little out of plumb and just for simple, easy opening. But the tighter the better while still being able to easily swing open or close, as tight produces a better seal to hold in heat.

1. Cut two vertical pieces of 2x2 each 70 3/4" with 90 degree cuts.

2. Cut two horizontal pieces each 35 3/4" with 90 degree cuts."

3. Use sheetrock screws to join these together and be sure to have your screws in tight, recessed slightly into the wood so they are not a hindrance to the door opening; and be careful to center your screws so you don't split the 2x2.

4. Cut four scrap 2x4's 6" long with 90 degree angles and install in all four inside corners using lath screws to stiffen and support door as shown in **Figure 10c**. If

Build the Door

Figure 10c

you come in from the outside of the 2x2 make sure the screw head is recessed so it does not interfere with the door opening. If you want to make your door more professional looking you can make 45 degree angle cuts on the four 6" 2x4's instead of 90 degree cuts.

5. Make a latch assembly of your choice. I used bent scrap pieces of metal and a bent can opener.

6. Use self-taping screws threaded through the end of nylon rope to make door handles on both sides of the door.

7. Cut and install with Grip-tites a piece of plastic sufficient in size to cover the opening and wrap around two 90 degree angles so it can attach on the inside.

Option: You can build a second door on the opposite side of the greenhouse if you desire or just wall it over with plastic. My experience shows that the second opening is helpful for ventilation on hot summer days but it doesn't have to be a

How to Build a 12 x 14 Hoop Greenhouse

framed door. I just cut a piece of plastic that overlapped 1' on each side of the opening, attached a 3' piece of 2x2 to the bottom with Grip-tites and then made it into a roll-up shade that could be tied off at any height as needed or sealed tight with Grip-tites in the winter.

INSTALL THE GFI ELECTIRCAL OUTLET, EMT CONDUIT & WIRING

Figure 11a

1. Find a suitable place in the greenhouse to locate the GFI outlet that ideally is

How to Build a 12 x 14 Hoop Greenhouse

Figure 11b

in line with the house outlet, and nail the metal box in place. Against one of the vertical 2x4 end supports is a good location as shown in **Figure 11a**.

2. Attach the metal conduit to the bottom of the box and extend down to the ground. **Do not** put a corner joint on at this time.

3. Dig a 6" deep trench from directly below your nearest house exterior outlet (**Figure 11b**) in a beeline to just below the GFI outlet in the greenhouse. It is possible to use an exterior outlet that is not a straight beeline to the greenhouse, but I would not recommend it as it will require a lot more trench digging and more angles in the underground metal conduit making threading the wiring that much more challenging.

4. Lay as many 10' sections of conduit pipe as needed to get the length required to go from underneath the house outlet to underneath the GFI outlet in the greenhouse. Put joints in place near each section, but **do not** attach the joints at this time.

Install the GFI Electircal Outlet, EMT Conduit & Wiring

5. Thread the insulated 3 wire electrical cord through the pipes from the first pipe underneath the house outlet to the end of the last pipe under the GFI outlet. Make sure you have sufficient additional cord sticking out of the end of the pipes to reach the outlets.

6. Attach the 90 degree elbow joints to the pipe on the ground at either end and thread the cord through the elbow joints.

7. Run the wire up to the GFI outlet and attach to electrical code. If you do not feel qualified to do this please call an electrician.

8. Attach the face plate to the GFI outlet with the screws provided.

9. Attach a plug to the end of the cord near the house and plug it in. You now have electricity to your greenhouse.

INSTALL THE ROLL-UP PLASTIC OVER THE HOOPS

Figure 12

How to Build a 12 x 14 Hoop Greenhouse

Note: A second person is necessary for this phase.

1. Spread out the plastic on the north side of the greenhouse. If there is even a little wind you will probably need to weight the corners down with lumber or rocks.

2. Using Grip-tites, attach the plastic along the north 14' Foundation Board. Try to keep it tight as you nail in the Grip-tites, and *remember to leave at least 2' extending onto the ground.* The perimeter hay bales will be sitting on this extended plastic.

3. Using two people, bring the plastic over the top of the ridge and drape down the south side.

4. Using Grip-tites, further attach the plastic on the **south side** by nailing into the diagonal supports on the end frames. *Do not attach the plastic with Grip-tites on the south side diagonals.*

5. Run the plastic out at least 2.5' over the ground on the south side and lay the 16' 2x2 across the plastic running the length of the greenhouse and extending 1' past the end of the greenhouse on both sides.

6. Curl the plastic at least one complete turn around the 2'x2'x16" and firmly attach it with Grip-tites through all the wraps of the 2x2. The wrapped 2x2 should be resting right at ground level and pulling the plastic tighter by its weight. 2' of overlapping plastic should be extended on the ground.

ATTACH THE GROMMETS & PLACE THE STRAW BALES

Figure 13a

The south side, which faces the daily transit of the sun, is the roll-up side. You can use Grip-tites to attach the plastic on the north side up to the ridge pole, but on the south side eye hooks and nylon cord will be used. To accomplish this you must install brass grommets in the plastic but ***this must be***

How to Build a 12 x 14 Hoop Greenhouse

Figure 13b

done correctly otherwise they will just rip out in the first wind storm.

Note: In *Figure 13b* the grommet on the left is installed correctly with a piece of high quality duct tape making it rip-proof. The incorrectly installed grommet on the right (without duct tape) already shows a rip in the plastic just to the right of the grommet despite a quadruple fold. Plus it was placed too close too the edge. Do it wrong and your plastic will look like the picture in *Figure 13c* after the first gust of wind.

1. Trim the plastic hanging off the east and west sides so there is enough hanging down to come at least midway into the triangle made by the diagonal supports/door frame/foundation boards on the End Frame.

2. Starting near the top of the door frame vertical, install one eye hook.

3. Now fold the nearest plastic over on itself and where you intend to place a grommet that will anchor to that eye hook with cord, take a 1' piece of high-quality, thick duct tape or Gorilla tape and place it over the plastic.

4. Punch a hole through the duct tape and plastic near the edge (about 1" away), just big enough to fit the grommet, where you intend to place the grommet, using

Attach the Grommets & Place the Straw Bales

Figure 13c

the hole punch from the grommet tool kit. (*see Figure 13b*)

5. Install the grommet with the grommet tools (*see Figure 13a*).

6. Repeat the procedure and install at least 5 grommets and eye hooks total as you go from top to bottom.

7. Place straw bales on the plastic and the 16' 2x2 on the south side. If the plastic was installed tightly with Grip-tites all around, the weight of the straw bales will make the whole roof very tight.

8. On each side fold the plastic back on itself as need to further tighten the plastic. You can use a common house stapler to staples these folds together as shown in **Figure 13b**.

9. Tie off one end of your nylon cord at the lowest eye hook on one side of the roll-up plastic. Then run the bitter end through the lowest grommet on the plastic. Weave it now over to the next highest eye hook then back to the next highest grommet. Continue until you are at the top pulling the plastic tight as you go. Tie off on the last eye hook.

10. Repeat the same procedure on the other end of the greenhouse. You now have a tight enclosed greenhouse. When you want to roll up the south side, either partially or all the way to the ridge pole, just quickly pull the cord out of the grommets, roll the straw bales on the south side forward off the plastic on the ground, roll up the plastic to the desired height, wrap the cord around the end of the 16' 2x2 and secure to the top eye hook. Although it sounds complicated it is a simple, one person operation that takes no more then 1-2 minutes per side.

11. Place the remaining straw bales around the perimeter of the greenhouse. Remember to place them on edge if you want them to remain dry and intact or on the flat side if you want them to absorb water and decompose in place.

12. If you live in a cold winter area you may want to build the north wall up 2 or 3 layers of straw bales and if that is done they should be put down on their flat side as they would be unstable on the edge side. If put on their flat sides they will decompose fairly quickly and you'll end up eventually with a soil berm. You cover them with some actual soil to speed up the process.

OPERATING YOUR GREENHOUSE

Figure 14

Figure 14 shows the temperature in my greenhouse on a sunny day in January when it was 40 degrees outside. I was lounging inside in my shorts reading a book.

Congratulations! You're ready to start growing delicious fruits, veggies and

How to Build a 12 x 14 Hoop Greenhouse

flowers as you desire. The tighter you keep the greenhouse the more it will retain both heat and humidity. In the winter you can add supplemental heat with a simple liquid-filled radiator style electric heater. Just be sure to keep it centered near the middle of the greenhouse and away from anything flammable. **Don't use space heaters that have exposed heating elements** and don't use non-electrical space heaters. Besides being a fire hazard they will use up all the oxygen in the sealed greenhouse and could produce toxic gases unless ventilated.

Even though you are using an exterior GFI outlet you should also cut and install a small piece of plastic over the top of the outlet to prevent any water dripping down from the roof. When your greenhouse is in humid mode a lot of water will condensate and drip down from the roof and the plug should be kept completely dry.

My greenhouse had no problem with 5 inches of snow or 40 mph winds. If you are worried about snow load you can always put up an internal vertical 2x4 near the center for extra support. If you do this just loop a piece of cord over the ridge pole and attach it to the top of the 2x4 with screws, pulling it up tight to the ridge pole. Cut the bottom to tightly fit the distance to the ground level in your greenhouse. For added security, I recommend digging a 6" deep hole and placing the bottom of the 2x4 in the hole, filling with dirt and then measuring to make it the right length to be tight against the ridge pole on top.

If you have a lot of wind in your area you can make the greenhouse more resistant by running support lines made from non-stretching rope, down at a 45 degree angle to the ground from the top of each end frame, and anchored to the ground with tent stakes.

If you want a bigger greenhouse you can extend the length as far as you want by adding additional foundation boards and ribs, but don't extend the width unless you use sturdier ribs.

Enjoy!

Jesse Love
Celestopea Engineering & Design
www.celestopea.com/Designs.htm

PS Be prepared. All your neighbors are going to be intrigued by your new greenhouse and you will probably get some requests to help them build one too. You are definitely going to have new popularity in the neighborhood especially when you share your March and November tomatoes!

ABOUT THE AUTHOR

I have been blessed with some amazing experiences in my life that certainly have influenced me to have a desire to help the people of the world. Many of my books penned under both Jesse Love and Embrosewyn Tazkuvel are written with that goal in mind. I've been fortunate to have traveled to many countries around the world and interacted with people from the president of the country to the family living in a shack with a dirt floor. Being among people of many cultures, religions and social standings, watching them in their daily lives, seeing their hopes and aspirations for their children and the joys they have with their families and friends, has continually struck me with a deep feeling of oneness. I've been with elderly people as they breathed their last breath and at the birth of babies when they take their first. It's all very humbling. This amazing world we live in and the wonderful people that fill it have given me so much. My books are my way to give back as much as I can to as many people as I can.

You can contact me through the "Contact Us" form on *www.celestopea.com*.

If you have enjoyed this book, I would be honored if you would take a few moments to visit the book page on Amazon and leave a review for the book.

CPSIA information can be obtained
at www.ICGtesting.com
Printed in the USA
LVOW03s1726250716
497700LV00011B/345/P